FLEX-ABILITY POPS

Solo-Duet-Trio-Quartet With Optional Accompaniment
Arranged by VICTOR LOPEZ

CONTENTS

	PAGE	CD TRACK FULL PERFORMANCE	CD TRACK ACCOMPANIMENT ONLY
B♭ Concert Tuning Note		1	
La Bamba	2	2	3
When the Saints Go Marching In	4	4	5
Eye of the Tiger	6	6	7
Peter Gunn	8	8	9
In the Midnight Hour	10	10	11
China Grove	12	12	13
Jeepers Creepers	14	14	15
Soul Man	16	16	17
Sweet Georgia Brown	18	18	19
Frosty the Snowman	20	20	21
Celebration	22	22	23

(0621B) OBOE/GUITAR/PIANO/BASS
(0622B) FLUTE
(0623B) B♭ CLARINET/BASS CLARINET
(0624B) ALTO SAX/BARITONE SAX
(0625B) TENOR SAX
(0626B) TRUMPET/BARITONE T.C.
(0627B) HORN IN F
(0628B) TROMBONE/BARITONE/BASSOON/TUBA
(0629B) VIOLIN
(0630B) VIOLA
(0631B) CELLO/BASS
(0632B) PERCUSSION
(0638B) CD ACCOMPANIMENT

Project Manager/Editor: Thom Proctor
Art Design: Ernesto Ebanks
CD MIDI Sequencing: Mike Lewis

© 2001 Alfred Publishing Co., Inc.
All Rights Reserved

LA BAMBA

MEXICAN FOLK SONG
Arranged by VICTOR LOPEZ

WHEN THE SAINTS GO MARCHING IN

TRADITIONAL
Arranged by VICTOR LOPEZ

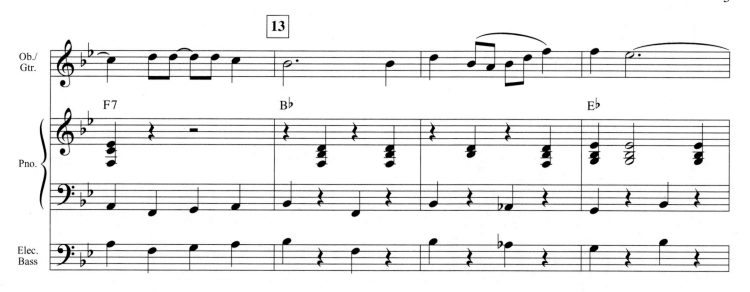

EYE OF THE TIGER
(Theme from "ROCKY III")

Words and Music by
FRANKIE SULLIVAN III
and JIM PETERIK
Arranged by VICTOR LOPEZ

PETER GUNN
(Theme Music from the T.V. Series)

Music by HENRY MANCINI
Arranged by VICTOR LOPEZ

IN THE MIDNIGHT HOUR

Words by WILSON PICKETT
Music by STEVE CROPPER
Arranged by VICTOR LOPEZ

CHINA GROVE

Words and Music by
TOM JOHNSTON
Arranged by VICTOR LOPEZ

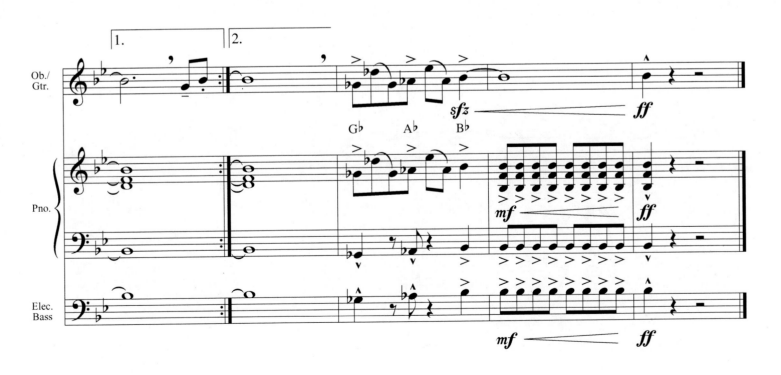

JEEPERS CREEPERS

Words by JOHNNY MERCER
Music by HARRY WARREN
Arranged by VICTOR LOPEZ

0621B

D.S. % al Coda

SOUL MAN

Lyrics and Music by
DAVID PORTER and
ISAAC HAYES
Arranged by VICTOR LOPEZ

0621B

SWEET GEORGIA BROWN

Words and Music by
BEN BERNIE, MACEO PINKARD
and KENNETH CASEY
Arranged by VICTOR LOPEZ

FROSTY THE SNOWMAN

Words and Music by
STEVE NELSON and JACK ROLLINS
Arranged by VICTOR LOPEZ

CELEBRATION

Words and Music by
RONALD BELL, CLAYDES SMITH, GEORGE BROWN,
JAMES TAYLOR, ROBERT MICKENS, EARL TOON,
DENNIS THOMAS, ROBERT BELL and EUMIR DEODATO
Arranged by VICTOR LOPEZ

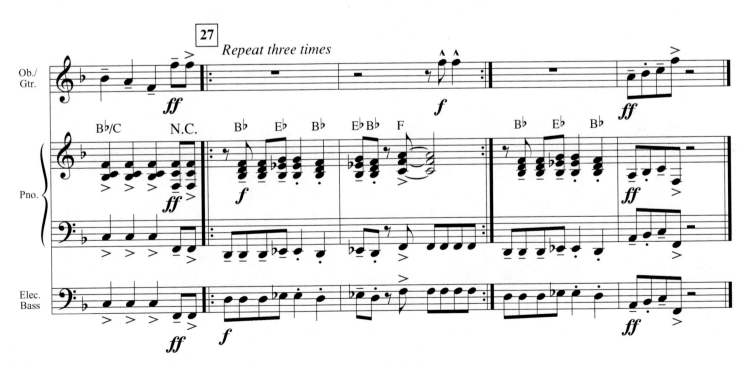

0621B